Oxford International Lower Secondary

8

English

Workbook

Emma Danihel
Mark Saunders

OXFORD

1 Crossing rivers

In this unit, you will do research and practise using different word classes, technical terms, descriptive language, comparatives and superlatives, and metaphorical language.

Transforming words

Nouns such as 'ingenuity', 'innovation', 'invention' and 'technique' can be transformed into a variety of word classes – adjectives, verbs and adverbs.

- Use the words from the list below to fill in the gaps in the sentences.

ingenious, ingeniously, ~~ingeniousness~~, ingenuity
innovate, innovation, innovative
invent, invention, inventor
technical, technicality, technically, technician

It was the ___ingeniousness___ of his plan that attracted the team to the project.

We are looking for an ______________ new product that will outshine our competitors.

Even the most elaborate and ______________ escape plan can go wrong.

A ______________ meant that the prisoner was released early from his sentence.

To ______________ means to come up with something new or make radical changes.

The idea was so ______________ simple that he wished he has thought of it first.

The computer was the most important ______________ of the twentieth century.

Digital media can bridge the gap between tradition and ______________.

In the laboratory, the ______________ was testing out a new kind of bio-fuel.

He liked to ______________ things, but most of them had little practical application.

Thomas Alva Edison was the ______________ of the light bulb.

The red team showed real ______________ to win the outdoor survival competition.

______________ speaking, there is little structural difference between the two bridges.

The engineer had a set of ______________ drawings showing the new bridge design.

Extension Write down the word class of each word you have used to fill in the gaps. Is it a noun, an adjective, an adverb or a verb?

Building vocabulary

You will need SB pp6–7

In this unit there are a lot of technical terms and descriptive words to explain the different types of bridges and what they are used for.

- Write your own definition of the following words which are connected to the topic of bridges.

pier/pile	a pillar, often cylindrical, supporting an arch
arch	
deck	
cable	

span	
support (weight)	
unstable	
vibration	

- Write a word that means the opposite of each of the words below.

stable		low	
vertical		weaker	
long		flexible	

- Choose the correct words from the list below to complete the sentences.

~~beam~~, construction, deck, location, suspension, truss, viaduct

A ____beam____ is a long, sturdy piece of timber or metal.

He wanted to know the precise ________________ of the Millau bridge.

A ________________ is another word for an elevated roadway or bridge.

To stop the rope bridge swinging they had to tighten the ________________.

He worked for a ________________ company that specialized in building bridges.

The ________________ framework of the bridge cast a pattern over the water.

A ________________ is another word for the road of a bridge or highway.

Describing bridges

- Below are pictures of three of the bridges on pages 10–11 of the Student Book. Write a description of each bridge. Make each description detailed and aim to capture what makes each bridge unique.

Extension Read one of your descriptions to a partner. See if they can guess which bridge you have written about.

Researching bridges

- Choose a bridge. It could be one you love or one you hate – a small bridge or a famous one. Find out what you can about the bridge by researching the answers to the questions below.

Geographical position
Where in the world is it? What water does it cross and what areas does it connect?

History
When was it built? Has it been re-built at any time?

Structure
What makes it strong? How is the weight distributed?

Importance
Is it an important landmark for the country? How does it benefit local people?

Extension Use your notes to write an information text about your chosen bridge.

Comparatives and superlatives

Regular adjectives are turned into the comparative by adding *-er* to the end of the word. They are turned into the superlative by adding *-est* to the end of the word.

Irregular adjectives don't follow these rules. They use the word 'more' placed in front of the adjective to make the comparative and the word 'most' to make the superlative.

- Highlight the comparative and superlative adjectives in the text below.

The Millau Viaduct is the highest and heaviest bridge ever built. It used construction and design techniques which did not exist even ten years ago. An even bigger bridge is planned to span the Straits of Messina between southern Italy and Sicily.

- Place the adjectives below into either the 'Regular' or 'Irregular' column. Then write the comparative and superlative forms for each.

delicate, elegant, famous, high, old, rigid, ~~strong~~, wide

Regular adjective	Comparative	Superlative
strong	stronger	strongest

Irregular adjective	Comparative	Superlative

- Choose the correct adjective from the list below to complete each sentence.

darker, fastest, harder, most difficult, most significant, older, oldest, quickest

The London Underground is the ________ underground train system in the world.

The Industrial Revolution in Europe was one of the ________ periods in bridge-building.

Irena was one year ________ than her sister Olga, but everyone thought they were twins.

The gold medallist had recorded the ________ time in the 100 metres freestyle.

Often, the ________ part of writing an essay is coming up with the opening sentence.

As the evening got ________. It became ________ to see the cricket ball.

Both sisters reached for the last cake, but Lucy was the ________ of the two.

Words starting with *auto-*

- Match each word starting with *auto-* with the correct definition.

autobiography	governing or acting independently
autocrat	a person's own writing, usually their signature
autograph	a car
automatic	a king or governor with absolute power
automobile	a self-written account of a person's life
autonomously	doing something without thought or attention, for example by a person or machine

- Use the above *auto-* words to complete the following sentences.

The fans waited at the entrance to the stadium hoping to get an ____________.

The garage door was ____________ and opened by remote control.

After retiring, the outgoing prime minister started to write her ____________.

Each of the new regions in the country was allowed to run itself ____________.

The country's leader, who opposed democratic reform, was an ____________.

Everyone rushed outside to watch the first ____________ in their town drive by.

The bridge as metaphor

Because a bridge is something everyone is familiar with, it is often used in a non-literal way. In English, there are many popular phrases that refer to bridges.

- Match each of the idioms below with its correct explanation.

It was like <u>a bridge over troubled water</u>.	putting off thinking about a problem that has not happened yet
It's all <u>water under the bridge</u> now.	an action or person that calms a difficult situation and offers a solution
We'll <u>cross that bridge when we come to it</u>.	causing offence and making it difficult to make amends
He's <u>burnt his bridges</u> now.	events that happened in the past and can now be forgotten about

Metaphors

Writers use metaphorical language to make their writing more exciting. When you describe something as if it were something else, it is called a metaphor. For example, 'her words cut deeper than a knife' (words are not sharp objects that can cut into anything), or 'he has a heart of gold' (a heart is a human organ, not an object of gold).

- Draw lines to match each metaphor with the correct definition.

You are a walking encyclopaedia.	You are active and energetic.
You are my sunshine.	You have a good character but not very good manners.
You have a heart of stone.	You are very dear, important.
You have a heart of glass.	You take little exercise and sit a lot.
You are a chip off the old block.	You are always busy and work hard.
You are a couch potato.	You are clever.
You are full of beans.	You know everything, are full of facts and figures.
You are a rough diamond.	You are just like or resemble a parent.
You are a bright spark.	You are affected easily; very easily upset.
You are a busy bee.	You have a cold, cruel personality.

Animal metaphors

To describe the personalities of human characters, writers often compare them to animals.

- What kind of human characteristic might each word or phrase describe?

chicken	someone who is very nervous, afraid of everything
book worm	
eel	
donkey	
lion	
monkey	
mouse	
night owl	
peacock	
snake	

2 Communication

In this unit, you will practise using abstract nouns, pairing verbs with prepositions, identifying adjectives and adverbs, and recognizing the literal and non-literal use of verbs.

Abstract nouns

Abstract nouns are used to label emotions and concepts.

- The sentence in the box describes Marcel Marceau's approach to mime. Highlight the six abstract nouns.

> Through the movements of his body he expressed everything – from beauty, comedy and conflict to despair, tragedy and hope.

- Separate the abstract nouns below into 'positive' or 'negative' meanings.

comfort, courage, deceit, disappointment, doubt, enthusiasm, envy, happiness, jealousy, love, melancholy, opportunity, pain, poverty, romance, sorrow, satisfaction, stupidity, trust, victory

Positive	Negative

- Match each abstract noun below with the correct definition.

belief →	having faith or trust in someone or something
childhood	a viewpoint held or conclusion reached
employment	something done for interest or amusement
entertainment	a job, career or occupation
failure	the early years of life before becoming a teenager
forgiveness	a thing or person that proves unsuccessful
imagination	a copy or likeness of something
imitation	the act of forgiving or pardoning someone
opinion	the destruction or surrender of something valued
sacrifice	the part of your mind that thinks creatively

Writing summaries

You will need SB pp21–22

- In the boxes below, write a summary of each paragraph from the text about Marcel Marceau on pages 21–22 of the Student Book. Try to use only half the number of words from each paragraph.

Paragraph 1: 'The greatest mime artist of modern times …'

Summary:
The greatest mime artist was known as the Master of Silence. Marcel Marceau was adored the world over and gave over 300 performances a year. This talkative man, who spoke five languages said, "Mime, like music, has neither borders nor nationalities."

Paragraph 2: 'At the age of five, in 1928, Marceau …'

Summary:

Paragraph 3: 'Mime has a long history …'

Summary:

Paragraph 4: 'In sixteenth-century Italy …'

Summary:

Paragraph 5: 'The art of silence …'

Summary:

Extension How did you find this technique of writing summaries? Write a paragraph reflecting on the experience and explaining whether you will use it when you take notes and research topics in the future.

Pairing verbs and prepositions

There are many prepositions in English. They often tell us where, when or how something happened.

- Circle the verbs and underline the prepositions in these sentences.

In the 1950s when he was at the height of his career, he gave 300 performances worldwide each year.

In silent films, the actors did not speak, but short written summaries of what was happening appeared on the screen for the audience to read.

When the Romans conquered Greece, they brought the Greek art of mime back to Italy.

The traditional Harlequin character was introduced to France in the 1570s.

- Find the correct preposition to fill each of the gaps below.

Marcel Marceau mimed a story __on__ stage.

Marceau began ________ imitate people, birds and even plants.

________ the movements of his body he expressed everything.

In ancient Greece mime was a form ________ theatre where scenes ________ everyday life taught moral lessons.

________ the time of Emperor Augustus of Rome, mime was very popular.

Marcel Marceau based his character Bip ________ the tradition of Pierrot.

Mime artists can be seen entertaining people ________ many city streets today.

Some earn money by making themselves ________ white statues.

- Complete the following sentences with the correct preposition.

about, against, for, from, into, ~~on~~, to, with

They all agreed __on__ a plan of action.

She looked ________ shells on the shore.

The children played ________ their dog.

They borrowed a ball ________ a friend.

He divided the cake ________ two pieces.

None of them had thought ________ it.

It belonged ________ the visiting team.

Several of them pushed ________ it.

Literal and non-literal verbs

Many verbs can be used for both a literal meaning and also to mean something non-literal, like the example of 'to touch'.

- Decide which of the following pairs of sentences demonstrates a literal use of the verb, and which is non-literal. Circle the verb.

They used a log to bridge the stream.	literal
The gamekeeper had to shoot the wounded deer.	
Time seemed to fly while they were at the fun fair.	
The car was stolen some time in the middle of the night.	
They were warned not to jump to any conclusions.	
His mind was racing with ideas after hearing the stirring speeches.	

They wanted to bridge the gaps in their knowledge.	non-literal
He began to shoot out some new ideas.	
She rushed up to the top of the hill to fly her kite.	
She stole a glance at the old castle ruin as they drove past it.	
The monkeys jumped up into the trees to escape.	
The athletes arranged to race each other on the track after school.	

- Write your own sentences using each of the non-literal verbs above.

They were able to bridge the gap between their ages through their mutual interest in ancient history.

Extension Many more verbs are used non-literally in English. Write a list of as many as you can think of.

Recognizing adjectives and adverbs

Adjectives and adverbs can take many different forms. Adjectives modify, or describe, nouns. Adverbs modify verbs to give more information about the actions.
For example:
'I finally succeeded.' (adverb)
'She was a good student.' (adjective)

- Read this extract from *The Story of My Life* (on pages 26–27 of your Student Book) and identify all the adjectives.

> I became impatient at her repeated attempts and, seizing the new doll, I dashed it upon the floor. I was delighted when I felt the fragments of the broken doll at my feet. I had not loved the doll. In the still, dark world in which I lived, there was no strong sentiment or feelings of tenderness.

- Identify the adverbs that are used to modify the verbs listed below the extract.

> As the cool stream gushed over one hand she spelled into the other the word 'water', first slowly, then rapidly. I stood still, my whole attention fixed upon the motions of her fingers. Suddenly the mystery of language was revealed to me.

spelled: ________; ________	stood: ________	revealed: ________

- Circle all of the adjectives and underline all of the adverbs in the extract below.

> The morning after my teacher came she led me into her room and gave me a doll. When I had played with it a little while, Miss Sullivan slowly spelled into my hand the letters d-o-l-l. I was at once interested in this finger play and tried to imitate it. When I finally succeeded in making the letters correctly, I was filled with pleasure and pride. Running downstairs to my mother I held up my hand and made the letters for 'doll'. I did not know that I was spelling a word or even that words existed; I was simply making my fingers go in monkey-like imitation. In the days that followed I learned to spell in this way a great many words, among them 'pin', 'hat', 'cup' and a few verbs like 'sit', 'stand' and 'walk'. But my teacher had been with me several weeks before I understood that everything has a name.

Extension Write a paragraph to describe a situation where you learned something completely new. It could have been in school or elsewhere. When you have finished writing, highlight the adjectives and adverbs.

Writing an account of an experience

- Read the lines below from the poem 'Touching' by Nissim Esekiel (on page 31 of your Student Book).

> We are touched
> By a film or a book.

- Write your own account of an experience that is linked to the lines above. In your writing, explore using verbs for their literal and non-literal meanings.

Extension Highlight any non-literal verbs you have used in your account.

Structure and features of autobiography

An autobiography tells the life story of the person writing it. As with writing any story, it is important to include details which the reader will find interesting and will help them to understand the experience being described.

- Read the following lines from Elephant Bill's autobiographical account of his encounters with the elephant, Ma Kyaw (you read about this on pages 33–34 of your Student Book).

> I treated her every day for three weeks. To begin with she suffered great pain and made a lot of fuss. But I was determined to treat her and she became a good patient.

- In the box below, write down any questions you would like to ask Elephant Bill to understand more about how Ma Kyaw became a 'good patient'.

- Use your questions above to help you to expand the lines from the extract into a full paragraph, adding the detail you felt was missing. Use descriptive language and specific detail to bring the experience alive for the reader.

Extension Highlight all the adjectives and adverbs you have used in your paragraph.

3 Feeding us all

In this unit, you will develop your vocabulary and writing skills, practise using *wh-* words (for questions) and writing haiku, and identify cause and effect clauses.

Vocabulary to describe amounts

The adjectives below describe amount. They are ranked in approximate order from the least to the greatest amount. These are useful words for discussing the availability of food.

- Write a sentence of your own using each amount word.

Least	rare	Fresh shellfish is a rare treat.
↓	meagre	
	sparse	
	insufficient	
	limited	
	small	
	adequate	
	sufficient	
	ample	
	plentiful	
	generous	
	abundant	
	substantial	
	copious	
	lavish	
Greatest	excessive	

- Use the words above to write several sentences about the sorts of food you eat in a week. Example: 'I eat ample fruit and copious amounts of green vegetables …'

Extension Circle the words in the table which can be started with a prefix. Examples are '<u>un</u>limited' and '<u>in</u>adequate'.

Food-related vocabulary

- Match each word with the correct definition.

Word	Definition
dairy	illness and death caused by a lack of sufficient food
diet	poor health caused by a lack of essential nutrients
fast food	the feeling of needing to eat more food
fibre	a person who does not eat meat
hunger	the range of food a person eats and their eating habits
malnutrition	food that is made from cows' or other animals' milk
processed	food that is produced and sold to people very quickly
starvation	roughage in the diet, from things like grain
vegetarian	describing food that has been prepared in a factory

Cause and effect sentences

The extract below is the first paragraph from the newspaper report about drought in Madagascar (page 38 of your Student Book).

Effect 2: Over one million people in Madagascar are struggling to get enough to eat

Effect 1: first famine

Cause: climate change

> Over one million people in Madagascar are struggling to get enough to eat, due to what could become the first famine caused by climate change, according to the World Food Programme (WFP).

- Summarize the causes and effects from the extract below by writing your own sentences.

> "However, climate change has upset the cycle, affecting smallholder farmers and their neighbours," said Alice Rahmoun, WFP Communications Officer, speaking to UN News on Thursday. "There is of course less rain, so when there is the first rain, they can maybe have hope and sow some seeds. But one little rainfall is not a proper rainy season," she said. "So there's not enough rain, so harvests fail constantly, so people have nothing to harvest and nothing to renew their food stocks and nothing to eat."

Climate change means that the weather cycle has changed.

Detail in newspaper reports

You will need SB p38

Newspaper articles and reports give factual details. They are often carefully written to make sure they answer most of the questions a reader might have about the event or story.

You can test how much real information an article contains by asking a range of questions using the *wh-* words. The *wh-* words are:

what, when, where, which, who, why, how

- Write a question using each of the above *wh-* words in response to the article on drought in Madagascar (page 38 of your Student Book).
- Then write your answer to each question, bringing out the key information from the article.

What does WFP mean?	World Food Programme
Why was WFP in Madagascar?	

Extension Use these question words to help you write a short report about something that is happening at your school or in your local area.

Wh- question words

- Write the most appropriate *wh-* word to complete each of the questions below.

Where did you go on holiday last year?

__________ do you know that Sam likes reggae music?

__________ do petrol combustion engines work?

__________ don't horses fall over when they sleep?

__________ is the next available appointment?

__________ factors hinder emergency aid relief?

__________ team do you think will win the world cup?

__________ is the head office located?

__________ many times a week do you go shopping?

Writing frequently asked questions (FAQs)

- Write four FAQs in the table below. Use the notes you made from your research on selected charities and organizations (for the task on page 40 of your Student Book) to write the answers.

Where is Oxfam based?	Oxfam GB is based in Oxford, UK. Oxfam International has member branches in 13 different countries.

Extension Highlight the *wh-* words that you have used in your FAQs and ensure that you have used as many different ones as possible.

Haiku syllables

Haikus follow the pattern of three lines. The first line has five syllables, the second line has seven syllables, and the last line has five syllables. A syllable is one of the individual sounds that form words.

- Identify how many syllables are in each of the words and phrases below.

zesty lime juice	
aromatic duck sauce	6
caramelized chocolate biscuits	
succulent buttered fish	
home-made tangy soup	

local delicacy	
Mediterranean vegetables	
hot and sour noodles	
sun-dried tomatoes	
velvety smooth mousse	

Writing a haiku

- Use the space below to draft ideas for your own haiku about food.

- When you have finalized your haiku, write it out as individual syllables in each of the spaces below to check it fits the rule (5, 7, 5).

Extension Work out the number of syllables in words from your own language, or another language you are learning. Do they sound different to English syllables?

Creating atmosphere

- Note the verb phrases and noun phrases that are used to create atmosphere in the extracts from 'Boggle Mill' below (from pages 43–45 of your Student Book). Decide which category they best fit into: sights, sounds, smells or feelings.

The man spoke quickly and took them both into a large kitchen. A fire lit the whole room with a warm orange glow and scented the house with a smoky fragrance. There was a strong, sweet smell of fruitcake, and baking bread.

Rueben had noticed the dirt on the children's boots, the stains and mud on their faces, and most of all their look of unease. His deep voice and broad accent made him sound like a stranger to that part of the world.

Sights: a large kitchen	Sounds:
Smells:	Feelings:

Describing your favourite food

- Use the space below to write a descriptive passage on your own favourite food. Use a wide and vivid vocabulary to describe the food. Use sight, sound, taste, feel and smell to create a vivid picture. Make the food sound very tempting.

Planning a story

You are going to plan a story about getting to know someone who at first seemed very different to you. Focus on how you changed your mind about them. What was the turning point at which you became friends?

- Plan your story by making notes in response to the prompts below.

The setting Give the time and place. What are the circumstances in which you met?	
Character 1 (the narrator) The person telling the story. Write your narrative in the first person ('I'). Give a brief account of your age and background.	
Character 2 Describe your first impressions of the person. What was it that set them apart? Write in the third person ('he' or 'she').	
Turning point How did your perceptions of the person change when you got to know them better? What was the turning point at which you became friends? At what point, do you start using the personal pronoun 'we'?	
Outcome How did the experience of meeting the person change you? What further insights did you gain into understanding cultural differences?	

Extension Write your story in full, giving it a title.

4 Health

In this unit, you will develop your vocabulary, design a book cover, practise using adjectives and adverbial phrases, and write instructions, descriptions and letters.

Using adverbials of frequency

- Write sentences about your daily life and routines using each adverbial of frequency.

always	I always eat breakfast before going to school.
annually	
daily	
never	
normally	
occasionally	
often	
rarely	
regularly	
sometimes	
usually	

Writing in the imperative

To form the imperative, you turn a sentence into a command, putting the main verb first. Example: 'Take a jar of clean water.'

- Change the sentences below to turn them into the imperative.

Level teaspoons must be used.	
The solution will need to be well mixed.	
It is important to boil the water you use.	
No more than 1 litre should be used in the rehydration solution.	

Writing instructions

You will need SB p54

In addition to using the imperative verb form in instructions, there are several other features to consider.

- Write a copy of your salt and sugar water instructions in the box below. Use the checklist to make sure you have included all the relevant features.

	☐ imperative sentences ☐ adverbials of time (for example, 'firstly') ☐ adverbs to connect clauses (for example, 'then') ☐ numeral adjectives (for example, 'two') ☐ chronological order

Describing a bicycle

- Write two paragraphs about a bicycle. In the first paragraph, describe the bicycle and its various features. In the second paragraph, write about some of the uses of a bicycle, such as riding to school, delivering pizza, or acting as an ambulance.

Extension Write a set of instructions for carrying out a particular maintenance task on a bicycle (for example, repairing a punctured tyre).

Adjectives used as nouns

Some adjectives in English can be used as nouns. For example, there is a saying in English that 'fortune favours the brave.' In this case, the word 'brave' is used as a plural noun, referring to a group of people who share this quality.

- Write sentences below, using the adjectives as nouns.

lucky	
hungry	
rich	
sick	
weak	

- The adjectives below can all be turned into nouns by adding a suffix to them. Connect the adjectives below with the correct suffix. Some words need to be altered before adding the suffix. Example: 'dens(e)' + *-ity* becomes 'density'. Write the full nouns in the third column.

careless
difficult
efficient
free
intense
just
violent
warm

-y	
-th	
-ce	
-ness	carelessness
-ity	
-cy	
-ice	
-dom	

Turning nouns into adjectives

- Turn the nouns below into adjectives. Then use each one in a sentence.

respectability, obligation, obsession, pomposity

Vocabulary and lexical fields

You will need SB pp58–59

A lexical field is a particular topic and all the words that relate to it.

- Find words from the text 'A visit to the bone-setter' that fit in each of the lexical fields below (see pages 58–59 of your Student Book).

Pottery	ceramics,
The human body	
Medicine	

Revising adverbs

You will need SB pp58–59

Several adverbs are used to describe the events in 'A visit to the bone-setter' in more detail.

- Find the adverbs in the text and write out the phrases.

hurt badly,

Vocabulary: borrowed words from Persian

- Write down the meanings of eight of the English words below that have been borrowed from Persian (Farsi), a language used in Iran and Afghanistan.

aubergine, azure, caravan, checkmate, jackal, jasmine, khaki, kiosk, lemon, lilac, lime, ounce, pistachio, pyjama, rhubarb, rice, sash, scarlet, shawl, spinach, talc, tambourine, tiger

Sentence order

You will need SB pp64–65

- The sentences in the paragraph below come from *The Village by the Sea*. They have been jumbled up. Put numbers in the boxes to show the correct order. You will have to pay close attention to the meaning of the sentences and the detail they give. Then check to see if your version matches the original text on pages 64–65 of the Student Book.

Instead, he ordered them to build a fire.	
When the fire had died down, he poked at it with a long stick, scattering the ashes so that they cooled.	
Once the fire had started crackling, he flung in packets of flowers that he took from a bag on the cow's back – jasmine, marigold, hibiscus and frangipani.	
He got up quickly and started being very busy.	
Then he went in to see their mother at last.	
He wanted a particular kind of wood and the sticks had to be laid just so.	
Then he scooped them up into his hand and asked for water.	
To their surprise he did not go in to see their mother as they had expected he would.	
He poured a little into the palm of his hand and with one thumb and forefinger he mixed it with the ash.	
The man looked at her with his sharp, bright eyes.	

Recognizing sentence types

- All four sentence types are used in the extract from *The Village by the Sea*. Match each sentence type to the correct example.

Statement	The medicine-man was near!
Exclamation	Have you any medicine for fever?
Imperative	The man looked at her with his sharp, bright eyes.
Question	Sweep up all that ash.

Extension Write sentences of your own of each type listed above.

Writing Bela's letter to her friend

- Imagine you are Bela, one of Lila's younger sisters in *The Village by the Sea*. You want to write a letter to your friend Adeela, who has moved away to the city, telling her about your impressions of the medicine man's visit. Set the letter out fully, with the date and a salutation. Use the prompts to help you include everything in the letter that you need to say.

[date] [address or letterhead] [salutation]
Describe the situation of Bela and her family.
Tell Adeela what the medicine man was like and what he did.
Explain Bela's biggest concerns and worries.
In a conclusion, describe what Bela thinks will happen next. What reassurance might Bela seek from her friend?
Close the letter and sign off.

Extension Check your letter and then write it up as a final draft.

Designing a book cover

- Choose a book that you have read and design a new cover for it. Use the two boxes below to illustrate the front and back covers and add the necessary text and publication details. On the front cover, include the title, the author's name and an appropriate picture. On the back cover, remember to include a summary of the book, the price and publisher's details, and a quotation from a reviewer/reader.

Extension Swap your cover with a partner. Decide if it sounds like a book you would like to read. Share what you liked about it and one suggestion to make the cover even better.

5 New pastures

In this unit, you will develop your vocabulary, practise using dynamic and stative verbs, verb infinitives, and prepositional phrases, and write comparisons and interview clips.

'No', 'not', 'nothing' and 'never'

You can use a range of words like 'no', 'not', 'nothing' and 'never' to express the opposite meaning of a particular word or the sense of a sentence. This is called negation.

- The sentences below are from the extract 'Arriving in London' on pages 70–71 of your Student Book. Underline the words and phrases that create negation in each of them.

London looked like nothing that I had ever seen.

In fact, the weather was fine and sunny and, although we did not know it then, quite mild for the time of year.

I had never seen such greenness in my life.

Our house was one of a row of almost identical houses stuck to each other on both sides, 'terraced', the English called it, and nothing like our 'detached' house in Jerusalem.

My mother had been accustomed to our stone villa with its tiled floors and open veranda, and this cramped house with its wooden floorboards and small rooms did not appeal to her.

Backing onto the scullery wall was an outside toilet, which was not now in use.

In no time, and despite England's cold weather, my mother removed the carpets which covered the kitchen and the hall and had the floor laid with reddish, brown shiny tiles ...

Upstairs there were no carpets and the floor was covered in linoleum.

- Below are some other sentences from the same extract that do not contain negation. Rewrite them to include a range of negation types.
  cannot, ~~never~~, not

They said it always rained in London.	They said it never stopped raining in London.
I was overwhelmed by the strangeness.	
I try to remember now when I first saw our new home in London.	

Extension Write a list of negative words that start with the prefixes *non-*, *no-* and *never-*.

Dynamic and stative verbs

Some verbs are used for physical actions, for example, 'to walk'. Some are used for things that are not physical, for example, 'to dream'. Physical verbs are called dynamic verbs and the other kind are stative verbs.

- Identify the 'dynamic' and 'stative' verbs in the following sentence from 'Arriving in London'.

I remember thinking when we were in the taxi driving towards our house that all the cars were driving on the wrong side of the road.

Sometimes the way in which a verb is used can determine whether it is stative or dynamic. For example, 'She felt the animal's broken leg carefully' is dynamic, but 'She felt unhappy about losing her wallet' is stative.

- Write a sentence of your own for each of the verbs below. Add if it is dynamic or static.
to compare, to know, ~~to prepare~~, to rain, to stand, to struggle

Joel mentally prepared himself for his first ever sky-dive.	stative

Words starting with *over-*

- Match each word starting with *over-* with the correct definition.

overcook	to have a strong emotional effect
overestimate	to leave in or on the oven for too long
overflow	to give someone too much money
overload	to flood or fill up beyond capacity
overpay	to put too much on something or someone
overwhelm	to give something too high a value

Extension Write a list of other words with the prefix *over-*.

Writing a comparison of two places

Use the spaces below to write a comparison of two different places that you know well (for example, your grandparents' home and your English classroom).

- Attach photographs or sketch pictures of the two places that you are comparing and answer the questions in the second column to structure your writing.

Photo 1	• What are the main differences between the two places? • What are the main similarities?
Photo 2	• How does each place make you feel? Which place do you prefer?

Extension Highlight the stative verbs and dynamic verbs you have used above, using two colours.

Verb infinitives

Infinitives are formed by placing the word 'to' before the root form of a verb (also called the base form).

- Underline the infinitive verb forms used in the poem 'Tent #50 (Song of a Refugee)' on page 75 of your Student Book.

> Tent #50, on the left, that is my present,
> But it is too cramped to contain a future.
> And, "Forget!" they say, but how can I?
> Teach the night to forget to bring
> Dreams showing me my village
> And teach the wind to forget to carry me
> The aroma of apricots in my fields!
> And teach the sky, too, to forget to rain.
> Only then may I forget my country.

A verb in the infinitive form cannot be the main verb in a sentence. This means that infinitives need to be used with an additional, finite verb that shows tense, person and number. For example, in the poem above, the verb 'cramped' is used before the infinitive 'to contain'.

- Complete each sentence opening below by adding an infinitive verb and an ending for the sentence.

The referee wanted … to abandon the match because of the poor weather.

Members of the government voted …

One day, global warming is going …

The DJ began …

Some of the students needed …

- Write sentences using the finite form of the first verb and the infinitive form of the second verb.

ask, sing	The girl asked to sing a solo.
buy, make	
cross, catch	
design, carry	
fly, travel	
give, play	
start, clean	

Prepositional phrases

Prepositions are used to express the relationship between a noun or pronoun and another word. For example, the preposition 'on' in the sentence, 'The mug is on the table', states where the mug is in relation to the table. A prepositional phrase includes the words that provide more information about the preposition.

- Complete the table below by adding either the relevant prepositional phrase or a sentence using the phrase given.

behind you	Harvey is the boy sitting behind you on the third row.
	The house will go under the hammer next week.
after dark	
	Abigail never arrives on time for her lessons.
during the concert	

- Tick the words below that can be used as a preposition in English. Research words you are unsure of.

about	☐	our	☐	past	☐
can	☐	near	☐	over	☐
between	☐	except	☐	do	☐
that	☐	spin	☐	since	☐
outside	☐	within	☐	from	☐
unlike	☐	despite	☐	because	☐

- Use at least six of the prepositions above in a piece of writing below.

Contractions

A common practice in speech is to contract words by taking out letters and even combining words together in a shorter form. When written, an apostrophe is used to show where letters have been omitted.

- Write out the full phrase for each of the following contractions.

can't	
wouldn't	
you'd	
isn't	
we're	
I've	
you'll	

we've	
you're	
I'll	
couldn't	
they're	
I'd	
mustn't	

Preparing to write an interview clip

- Find someone to interview who has moved from one area or country to another.
- Prepare for the interview by writing five questions you would like to ask the person. Write questions that will encourage them to talk.
- During the interview, make notes on the responses to each question.

Questions	Notes
What do you miss most about the place you moved from?	

Writing an interview clip

- Use your notes from conducting the interview to write the first draft of your interview clip.

6 Setting the scene

In this unit, you will write a playscript and practise using rhyme schemes, sentence subjects and objects, descriptive vocabulary and past participles.

Dramatic verbs

- Write definitions for each of the verbs below.

to terrify	to fill someone with terror and make them very afraid
to frighten	
to shiver	
to comfort	
to promise	
to fear	

Planning a script

You will need SB pp85–88

- Use the space below to plan a script of what might happen immediately after the *Great Expectations* scene on pages 85–88 of the Student Book.

What happens next?	**Notes**
Characters present in the scene • Pip is an orphan living with his sister. • Mrs Joe Gargery is Pip's sister. She resents her brother and is not very kind to him. • Joe Gargery is married to Pip's sister. He is gentle and kind towards Pip.	
Plot • Pip goes home to his sister and her husband. His sister is cross that he has been out so long. Pip secretly tries to take some food and a file to give to Magwitch.	
Setting • Christmas Eve, 1812 • Kitchen at the Gargery home	

Writing a script

- Now write your playscript using dramatic language. Don't forget to also write the stage directions. Aim to write at least five lines of dialogue for each character.

Extension Imagine that you are the director of a theatre performance of *Great Expectations*. What instructions would you give to the actors playing Pip, his aunt and his uncle? What costumes would they wear?

Rhyme scheme, repetition, alliteration and sibilance

- Underline the two pairs of lines from the poem 'The Listeners' (on page 91 of your Student Book) that rhyme with each other.

> 'Is there anybody there?' said the Traveller,
> Knocking on the moonlit door;
> And his horse in the silence champed the grasses
> Of the forest's ferny floor;
> And a bird flew up out of the turret,
> Above the Traveller's head:
> And he smote upon the door again a second time;
> 'Is there anybody there?' he said.

- Write two further lines of your own for the poem that rhyme.

Repetition in a poem can take many forms and cause a variety of effects. Sometimes, individual words are repeated. The structure of a particular line or phrase, or a particular image, may also be repeated.

- Identify and explain two more examples of repetition from 'The Listeners'.

Is there anybody there?	This phrase is repeated in full at the beginning and end of the poem, and creates a frame for the poem.

Alliteration and sibilance are other devices used by poets and writers to create particular effects. Alliteration is the repetition of consonant sounds, for example, the 'h' sound in '**H**ungry **h**ippo **h**ad a **h**uge **h**elping of **h**addock'. Sibilance is the repetition of the 's' sound, as in 'The **s**nake **s**lithered away in the **s**ilver mi**s**t'.

- Find an example of both devices in 'The Listeners' and explain their effects.

Alliteration	
Sibilance	

Writing an imaginative poem

- Write an exciting beginning to your own poem in the style of 'The Listeners', establishing an engaging and imaginative setting and characters.
- Use the checklist below to help you focus on dramatic opening lines, the mood and atmosphere, and the use of poetic devices.

Poetic devices ☐ use of repetition/alliteration ☐ rhyme schemes ☐ a question	
Characters ☐ memorable introduction ☐ essential details ☐ first, second or third person pronoun	
Setting ☐ time and place ☐ landscape features ☐ building (interior) details ☐ colours, sounds, smells	
Language ☐ emotive verbs ☐ noun phrases ☐ positive/negative words	

Extension Continue your opening to develop your piece into a complete poem.

Sentence subjects and objects

Subjects and objects are the 'things' in a sentence that are involved with the verbs and what is happening.

Usually subjects are the person or thing that is doing the verb. For example, in the sentence 'The courier brought the parcel', the subject is 'the courier'.

Objects are people or things that have things done to them. For example, in the sentence above, 'the parcel' is the direct object.

Subjects and objects are made up of nouns, noun phrases or pronouns.

- Identify the subjects and objects in each of these simple sentences from 'Mister Salgado'.

	Subject	**Object**
My friend answered the phone.	My friend	phone
His uncle pulled his ear.		
She slammed the door and stormed off.		
We shared Katie's packed lunch.		
I went to school yesterday.		

The following more complex sentences contain more than one subject or object. You can often find the direct object by asking what or who was affected by the subject. The first two sentences come from the extract 'Mister Salgado' on pages 93–95 of your Student Book.

- Underline the main subject and the main verb in each sentence and circle the main object.

You must do whatever he tells you.

When the sun sank behind the rooftops, we were summoned by a voice from somewhere deep inside the house.

My cousin, who lives in a flat in Milan, invited me to stay with him over the summer holiday.

I lent my notes to my partner as he was going to write up our project.

I wore my favourite top to the party which Judy threw at her mum's house.

Adding description with present and past participles

You will need SB pp85–88 & 93–95

A past participle refers to a past or completed action. It is usually formed by adding -*ed* to a verb. Similarly, a present participle refers to present action and is usually formed by adding -*ing* to a verb. Both can be used adjectivally, to add description to a person or thing.

- Copy the descriptive phrases in the extract from 'Mister Salgado' that contain the following past participles. (See pages 93–95 of the Student Book.)

crumpled		thatched	
spoken		untroubled	

Stage directions often use descriptive participles to describe the actions and emotions of the characters.

- Find more examples of past and present participles in the stage directions in *Great Expectations*. (See pages 85–88 of the Student Book.)

Pip	(terrified)	**Magwitch**	

Writing a dialogue

- Write your own dialogue for a meeting between two characters. Use descriptive participles for the stage directions.

Writing an article for a web page

The article on shadow puppetry (page 98 of your Student Book) is written in paragraphs to deliver four main pieces of information. The structure of each paragraph starts with a topic sentence and then gives more specific information. The first paragraph can be broken down like this:

Focus of paragraph	Topic sentence	Notes on extra detail
The history of shadow puppetry	Shadow puppetry is considered the oldest form of puppetry in the world.	Chinese, Southeast Asian, Turkish and Greek examples; 1800s in Western Europe; Lotte Reiniger

- Plan three paragraphs for an article on a subject that you would like to write about.

Focus of paragraph	Topic sentence	Notes on extra detail

Extension Write your own web page article from your plan, adding a title and including all the detail in each of the paragraphs.

Planning a shadow puppet play

- Plan the plot for your own shadow puppet play. Draw a rough outline of the characters and two scenes in silhouette in the boxes below.

Writing a shadow puppetry scene

- Base your script on the above scenes and characters. Write the dialogue for the first scene below. Then add any stage directions in italics in brackets.

Extension Write the dialogue for the remaining scenes of your play.

7 Peace

In this unit, you will develop your vocabulary, explore figurative language, practise using transitive and intransitive verbs, concrete and abstract nouns, produce a graphic novel and write poetry.

Phrasal verbs

The poem 'Don't Believe in War' contains the phrasal verb 'believe in', which means to have faith in a particular person or thing. You read this poem on page 102 of you Student Book.

- Find out the meanings of the following sets of phrasal verbs.

to back	to back down	to stop arguing your own side of something
	to back out	
	to back up	
to call	to call for	
	to call off	
	to call on	
to eat	to eat up	
	to eat in	
	to eat out	
to fall	to fall behind	
	to fall off	
	to fall out	

Metaphors and similes

You will need SB p102

Figurative language often combines literal and non-literal ideas, or associations. For example, the word 'exposed' from the poem 'Don't Believe in War' has a literal meaning of someone or something being visible, or out in the weather. (See page 102 of the Student Book.) Further associations include vulnerability, being caught out or abandoned to chance.

- Explain the associations created by the use of these words in the poem.

beneath	
mighty	
constricts	

Extension Look back at the poem and discuss how these associations affect its meaning.

Transitive and intransitive verbs

You will need SB pp104–106

If a verb is transitive, it needs a related object to make sense fully. In contrast, the action described in intransitive verbs makes sense without a related object.

For example, the first lexical verb in 'The Drop of Honey' is 'eat'. (See pages 104–106 in the Student Book.) This verb is transitive when part of the sentence 'There was once a king who was eating his breakfast.' The phrase 'his breakfast' is the related object.

However, the next verb 'sit' is intransitive. This is because it is followed by a prepositional phrase 'on one of his many balconies' rather than by an object.

- Find each of the transitive and intransitive verbs in 'The Drop of Honey' and copy out the phrase it appears in. For the transitive verbs, underline the related object.

to like	
to pour	
to fall	
to dart	
to fight	
to destroy	

Extension Write some sentences of your own using the verbs above, adding objects where required, to practise using transitive and intransitive verbs.

Titles and capital letters

- Decide whether the words for titles in each of these sentences need to have a capital letter or not. Write the correct form in each gap.

princesses	All the other ______________ were jealous of Lucilla and her beautiful dress.
prime minister	When the election day came, the people voted for a new ______________.
general	The seventh battalion received orders from the ______________ to advance.
officer	The whole police station threw a party for __________ Bowers when he retired.

Making a storyline

You will need SB pp104–106

- Use the space below to create your storyline for the events in 'The Drop of Honey'. The first and last events have been included, so you just need to record what happened in the correct order of events. Include 10 more events.

- The king dropped some honey from his balcony while breakfasting.

- Civil war broke out and destroyed the country.

Producing a graphic novel

Graphic novels are made up of a series of individual frames that capture a stage or development in a story. Use the storyline that you have created for 'The Drop of Honey' to produce a section of a graphic novel.

- From your storyline, choose two of the events that are next to each other. Illustrate the two frames to show how that part of the story developed. Use the checklist below to see if you can produce some particular effects that capture what is going on in the story.

Try to:

- [ ] Show movement, for example, of the action of the fighting crowd.
- [ ] Use bold colours to make different parts and characters stand out clearly.
- [ ] Make it clear how the two frames are related to each other.

- Add text in the box below each picture to explain what is happening in that part of the story.

Extension Design frames for all the events on your storyline and put them together as a complete graphic novel.

Planning a war poem

Look at the painting, *The Mule Track*, below. You are going to plan a poem about it.

The Mule Track, painted by Paul Nash

- Complete the boxes below with words and phrases that describe what is happening in the painting. Write about what you can see (especially the colours), hear, feel, smell and taste.

See	
Colours	
Hear	
Feel	
Smell	
Taste	

Writing a war poem

- You are now going to write your poem called 'The Mule Track'. First decide what tone your poem will have. For example, do you think the scene depicted in *The Mule Track* is exciting, terrifying or incredibly sad? Whatever you think, make that the mood of your poem. Use some of the words and phrases you identified on page 49 in your poem.

Concrete and abstract nouns

Nouns for things you can touch are known as concrete nouns. Abstract nouns represent a concept or emotion, which you cannot touch.

- Write the nouns below in the correct column.

courage, crane, death, family, friend, girl, hope, inspiration, legend, money, monument, paper, peace, project, statue, symbol, victim, weapon, wish

Concrete	Abstract

Creating your own image of peace

You are now going to plan your own image of peace. It could be a monument, symbol or cartoon. Make it personal to you or your country.

- Fill in the table in support of your proposal for a monument, symbol or cartoon.

Person or event chosen to represent peace	
Main ideas connected with the person or event	
Rough sketch of the monument, symbol or cartoon	
Paragraph explaining the main ideas	

Peaceful words

- Write down words and phrases that you associate with a peaceful world. They can be literal or non-literal phrases, a feeling or a fact. You could think about a peaceful painting you have seen to help you.

8 Looking back

In this unit, you will develop your vocabulary and use of punctuation, practise using irregular noun plurals and different sentence types, and write a composition.

Vocabulary starting with 'heart'

- Match each 'heart' word or phrase with the correct definition.

Word or phrase	Definition
heart-beat	illness caused by the weakening of the heart
heart-broken	being cruel or uncaring
heartburn	an intimate conversation with another person
heart disease	a single cycle of the heart or a brief moment of time
heartless	a generous and good-natured person
heart rate	the central part of a tree's main trunk
heart-rending	the speed at which the heart is beating
heart-to-heart	something that causes feelings of anguish
heart-wood	a sharp pain felt in the chest
hearty	a state of extreme unhappiness and disappointment

- Describe the meaning and usage of the following phrases that use the word 'heart'.

Phrase	Meaning and usage
to have your heart in your mouth	describes being in a state of anticipation or fear of what might happen, in a particular situation
to wear your heart on your sleeve	
to be all heart	
to know in your heart of hearts	
to learn by heart	

Extension Write down a list of words that include 'heart' and a hyphen. Example: 'cold-hearted'.

Filling your heart

You will need SB pp119–120 & pp125–126

- Use the heart shape to collect phrases that you can use in your own writing after reading each of the texts on pages 119–120 and 125–126 of the Student Book.

Irregular noun plurals

The word 'memory' is an irregular noun in the singular form. The plural form is 'memories'. There are various other ways that irregular noun plurals are formed.

- Put each of the irregular nouns below into the correct rule for its plural form.

analysis, ~~antenna~~, appendix, cactus, child, crisis, curriculum, fish, formula, foot, goose, index, phenomenon, radius, sheep, species, synopsis, tooth, woman

-a to *-ae*	antenna
change to *-a*	
add *-en* /*-ren*	
-is to *-es*	
-x to *-ices*	
no change	
-oo- to *-ee-*	
-us to *-i*	

Extension Find more irregular noun plurals and make a reference list in your notes.

The habitual past

- The verbs ‘used to’ and ‘would’ can be used to describe things in the past that happened often. ‘Would’ is slightly more formal than ‘used to’ but both are perfectly acceptable. Write sentences of your own using both forms.

would	
used to	
would	
used to	

Making a Venn diagram

- Use the Venn diagram to make notes on how a place you know well has changed since you were younger (for example, your neighbourhood or your school). Put ways in which it has not changed in the overlapping section of the circle.

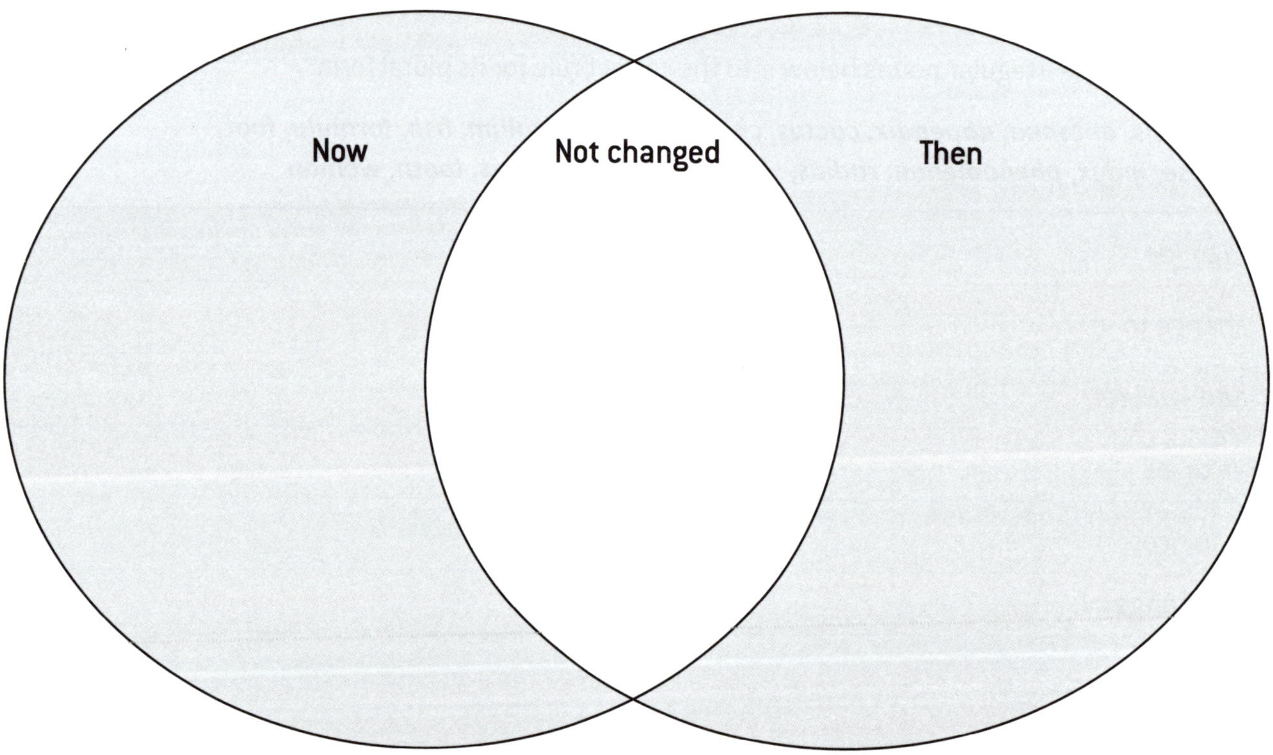

Extension Use your notes to write three paragraphs on the changes which have occurred in your chosen place.

The names of months

- Decide which month of the year matches each of the following descriptions.

perhaps named after Aphrodite, or the word *aperire* in Latin, meaning 'to open'	
named after Julius Caesar	
named after Mars, the god of war	
named after Maia, a Roman goddess	

Revising sentence functions

- Identify the four different sentence functions in the sentences below.

Tip

The sentence functions are **statement**, **exclamation**, **question**, and **imperative**.

It was a beautiful, mild morning.	
"Wait for me!"	
Leave our home?	
I will never feel the same again!	

- Write a sentence for each sentence type below.

Simple	
Compound	
Complex	

Extension Highlight the verbs in the sentences above and any conjunctions used to join clauses.

Using semi-colons to connect independent clauses

You can use a semi-colon instead of a coordinating conjunction ('and', 'but', 'or', 'nor', 'for', 'so', 'yet') to join two closely related independent clauses. The group of words that comes before the semi-colon and the group of words that comes after the semi-colon should both be complete sentences. The two sentences should be connected in some logical way. Examples:

'Harvey is outgoing, loud and very funny. Jason is shy, quiet and likes his own company.'

coordinating conjunction

'Harvey is outgoing, loud and very funny **but** Jason is shy, quiet and likes his own company.'

semi-colon

'Harvey is outgoing, loud and very funny; Jason is shy, quiet and likes his own company.'

A capital letter is not used after a semi-colon unless it is needed for a proper noun. Examples:

'The first series was brilliant. The second series was boring.'

no capital letter

'The first series was brilliant; the second series was boring.'

- Rewrite each of the following sentences with a semi-colon.

We paid a lot of money for the holiday. We had a fantastic time.
Goldfish make very good pets and they do not cost a lot to feed.
I try out every year for the school football trials yet I'm never picked for the team.
I don't like chocolate. My grandmother always makes me a chocolate cake when I visit her.

- Complete the following two sentences which use semi-colons.

The lights went out at 9:30pm on the dot;
; he didn't get very far at all!

Noun modification

You will need SB pp125–126

- Highlight the words in the phrases below that modify the noun.

a beautiful, mild morning
the estate's glamorous black Packard
his elegant grey linen *jugori*

- Find the following nouns in 'Visiting Grandfather and Grandmother' on pages 125–126 of the Student Book. Write the words in the text that modify each one.

household	seaside, filled with cousins
road	
blossoms	
hill	
love	
things	
han-bok	
bun	
cousins	
walk	

Words containing 'heart'

In 'Visiting Grandfather and Grandmother', Myung-ja says 'My heart was too heavy.' The compound word 'heavy-hearted' means depressed or miserable.

- Write a definition for each of the following compound words.

big-hearted	
cold-hearted	
faint-hearted	
half-hearted	
light-hearted	

Planning and writing a composition

- Plan your paragraphs for your composition on an event that made a great impression on you. Make notes on the content of each paragraph.

Paragraph 1: (past tense) Notes on the background to the event	
Paragraph 2: (past tense) Notes on the event itself	
Paragraph 3: (present tense) Notes on how you feel about the event now	

- Write a draft of your composition below, using your paragraph plan.

Extension Rework your composition to produce a final draft with improved vocabulary and a variety of sentence types.

9 The hidden world of cats

In this unit, you will develop your vocabulary, practise using adjectival phrases, conditional clauses, and descriptive language, identify different sentence functions, and write a comparison and a web page.

Animal vocabulary

- Match each word below with the correct definition.

carnivore	animals that have very small populations
endangered	a person who illegally hunts and kills animals
habitat	the area an animal marks out as its own
herbivore	an animal that eats meat
mythical	an animal that hunts at night
nocturnal	a particular kind of animal
poacher	an animal that eats plants and vegetation
predator	the type of environment an animal needs to live in
species	things that are fantastical and made-up
tame	an animal living naturally, away from humans
territory	an animal that hunts and kills other animals
wild	an animal that is used to contact with humans

Fronted adverbial and adjectival phrases

To create emphasis, it is possible to put additional detail at the start (front) of the sentence, before the main subjects, objects or verbs appear. Examples: 'Native to much of eastern and southern Asia, the tiger is a predator and a carnivore.' *(fronted adjectival phrase)*

'Aside from great bulk and power, its most recognizable feature is its pattern of dark vertical stripes.' *(fronted adverbial phrase)*

- Rearrange the sentences to put an adjectival or adverbial phrase at the front.

The great herd of antelope wandered across the plains.	Across the plains, the great herd of antelope wandered.
An owl is an excellent predator, nocturnal and silent in flight.	
When the cheetah begins to run, agile and muscular, it rarely loses its prey.	
After hibernating, tired and weak, the polar bear searches for a meal.	

Describing tigers in art

- Use the space in the boxes below to write a descriptive paragraph about each work of art depicting tigers. Think about how the tiger is presented, their habitat and what techniques the painters have used to create an effect.

Surprised! (or *Tiger in a Tropical Storm*)
Ghazi riding a tiger

Surprised! (or *Tiger in a Tropical Storm*), painted by Henri Rousseau

Ghazi riding a tiger

Writing a comparison

- Write three points of comparison between the two works of art depicting tigers.

Surprised! (or *Tiger in a Tropical Storm*)	*Ghazi* riding a tiger
•	•
•	•
•	•

Art gallery feedback form

You will need SB pp134–136

- Complete the feedback form below, using your notes, to write about your favourite of the four paintings on pages 134–136 of your Student Book.

Your name:
Name of the work of art:
Why did this particular work of art make such an impression on you?
Why do you think tigers have been an important subject in art?

Extension Highlight the specific animal-related vocabulary you have used in your comparison and feedback form.

Participles as adjectives

The present and past participle forms of verbs usually end in *-ing* or *-ed*. These participles can be used to form words that work as adjectives.

Examples: 'a well-walked path'; 'a running horse'

- Underline (or highlight) the *-ing* and *-ed* words that are used as adjectives. One sentence has more than one.

Dogs protect villagers from man-eating tigers in the Sundarbans.

The forested area is home to a dwindling number of tigers.

Dog-training experts have been employed to train effective guard dogs from the shabby strays found scavenging in village bins.

The village people are hunting in the same areas as the protected tigers meaning that they often come in contact.

One project trains stray dogs to act as an alarm when any prowling tigers come too close to the villages.

Writing a fact file

- Plan a fact file for an endangered animal of your choice, using the prompts and checklist below.

Your chosen endangered animal:	Checklist:
Where the animals lives, what it eats, its size, weight … :	☐ Title ☐ Images ☐ Captions ☐ Clear, concise information ☐ Bullet points ☐ Facts and figures ☐ Specific, technical language ☐ Sections ☐ Some short, snappy facts as well as more detailed information
Wildlife conservation projects trying to help the animal:	
What the future looks like:	

Extension Produce a full draft of your web page from your plan.

Vocabulary: words in many forms

The adjective 'relieved' and the verb 'to relieve' are related to the noun 'relief'.

- Write out the different forms of each word below. For two words, there is no adverb form.

	Verb	Noun	Adjective	Adverb
condemn				
encourage				
kill				
moan				
protect				

- List as many words as you can that can be formed from the words below.

gratitude	communicate	forgive	enjoy	master
gratefulness				
grateful				
ungrateful				
ingratitude				
gratefully				

- Write a sentence with the adverb and adjective form of each of the words below.

gratitude	The grateful cat lapped up the saucer of milk. (adjective) He gratefully said 'thank you' for his present. (adverb)
communicate	
forgive	
enjoy	
master	

Revising imperatives

- Write a command in the imperative to go with each of the signs below.

	Keep your sunroofs closed in this area.

Using fronted conditional clauses

Conditional clauses are subordinate clauses that begin with the word 'if'. They state something that might be true or might happen if certain conditions are met. Conditional clauses can be placed at the start of a sentence (fronted) or later in a sentence, after the main clause.

- Rebuild the three complex sentences below about Elsa, the writer and the baboons. Match each main clause to the correct subordinate clause using a connecting line.

Subordinate clause	Main clause
If the monkeys swing too close,	the little baboon might have drowned.
If the writer hadn't started taking photos	Elsa tries to swipe them with her paw.
If the old baboon didn't come to the rescue	the lioness wouldn't have jumped on her.

- Write each pair as a sentence with a fronted conditional clause.

Extension Try rewriting each of your sentences with the main clause first. Think about the different effects created by the pairs of sentences.

Descriptive vocabulary

- Read this extract from *Born Free* (on pages 142–144 of your Student Book). Circle the words or phrases that describe the sounds the baboons make. Underline the movements or actions they make.

> As soon as I tried to concentrate I heard the inquiring bark of a baboon peeping through the foliage; then the bush on the opposite bank became alive with inquisitive watching faces. Soon, intrigued by Elsa, they came more and more into the open, swinging recklessly from tree to tree, screaming and barking, sliding backwards down the trunks or hopping and swaying like shadows in the treetops, until one little chap fell with a splash into the river. At once, an old baboon came to its rescue, and clutching the wet, struggling creature, raced off with it to safety. At this, all the baboons in the world seemed to have got loose and the screeching was deafening. Elsa, who could tolerate the noise no longer, plunged into the river and swam across, accompanied by the hilarious shrieks of the baboons.

- Choose one of the verbs below to complete each of the sentences describing the different animals' movements.

crawled, flew, floated, galloped, leaped, marched, slid, slithered, sprinted, swam

The ants ______________ across the jungle.	The horse ______________ over the sand.
The snail ______________ across the branch.	The cheetah ______________ after its prey.
The salmon ______________ upstream.	The thrush ______________ to its nest.
The snake ______________ under a stone.	The jellyfish ______________ in the sea.
The spider ______________ across its web.	The dolphin ______________ in the ocean.

- Which animals do you think make the following noises? Write your answer next to the noise.

growl	roar	purr	caw
honk	buzz	chirrup	croak
squeak	mew	bleat	screech
bark	cackle	grunt	meow
whinny	hoot	bawl	hiss
twitter	cluck	snarl	whoop

10 Survival: we can make it!

In this unit, you will develop your vocabulary, practise using the imperative and phrasal verbs, practise building suspense in narratives and use different methods to remember tricky spellings.

Word classes

- Complete the mind maps below by adding different suffixes and prefixes to make new words.

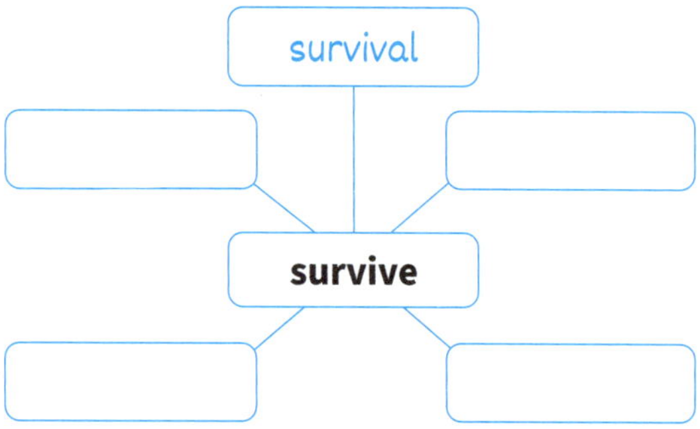

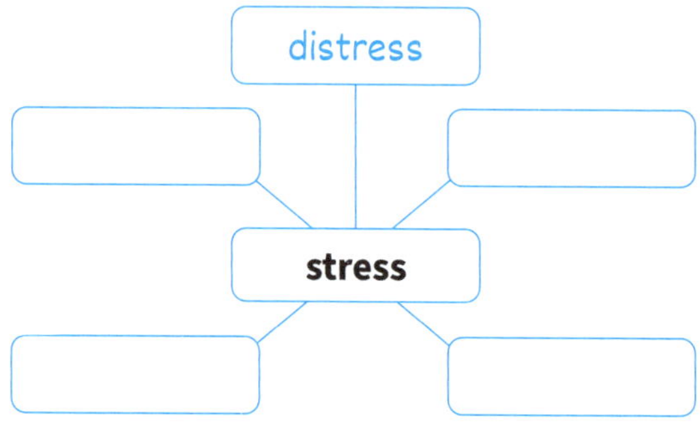

- Choose two more words from each mind map. Write each word in a sentence.

survival	The gladiator had to fight for his own survival.

Forming the imperative

To form the imperative, put the main verb first. It turns the sentence into a command. Example: 'Put your hat on.'

- Rewrite each sentence to create a command using the imperative form.

You should give your homework in on time.	
It's really important to use your best handwriting.	
You mustn't feed the zoo animals.	
Can you feed the chicken before you go out?	
If it's raining, I suggest wearing a raincoat when you go out.	

Extension See how many more words you can add to the mind maps above.

Giving advice using the imperative

The exam period is coming up at school. Your teacher has asked you to create a poster giving advice on how students can perform well.

- Write a list of five commands to give advice. Use the imperative form.
- Use each command as a subheading for your poster. Write one or two sentences in the box next to each command with further explanation.

Five ways to perform well in exams	Explanation
Get plenty of rest during the exam period.	

Extension Write five pieces of advice for a new student who wants to make friends with other students from your year.

Building suspense

- Continue the story below using as many ways as you can to build suspense, including giving hints about what is going to happen; not showing the reader all of the action; varying the length of words, sentences and paragraphs for effect.
- Then label the different techniques you have used.

Moonlight shone through the thin curtains at the window as Tawana sat bolt upright in her bed. She'd heard that noise again. She was sure of it. She sat straining to hear in the deafening silence.

short sentences

literary feature (oxymoron)

Extension Write the opening paragraph for a thriller. Use the techniques you have learned to build up tension in your writing.

Phrasal verbs

A phrasal verb is a phrase that combines a verb with a preposition, an adverb or both. It functions as a verb whose meaning is different from the combined meanings of the individual words. For example, 'give up' means to stop doing something.

- Match each phrasal verb with 'give' to the correct definition.

give away	stop doing something
give back	surrender
give in	return something
give up	reveal, often accidentally

- Complete each sentence below with one phrasal verb from above. Some verbs may need changing into the correct tense.

That's my pen. __________ it __________ now!
Sven ruined the film for everybody by __________ __________ the surprise ending.
We tickled Rebecca until she __________ __________ and told us where she had hidden the bag of sweets.
Maggie used to suck her thumb but she __________ __________ when her friends started teasing her about it.

- Match each common phrasal verb to the correct definition.

bring up	care for a child until adulthood
come across	invent a story
get on with	await something eagerly
look forward to	meet or find someone or something by chance
make up	used up, no more of
run out of	have a good, friendly relationship with

Extension Choose three common phrasal verbs and use them in your own sentences.

Tricky spellings: *-er* or *-or*

- Add the correct ending to each word below, using *-er* or *-or*.

jail_ _	garden_ _
anch_ _	profess_ _
labour_ _	climb_ _
sail_ _	adapt_ _
clean_ _	build_ _

Below is a list of 20 commonly misspelt words.

- Look quickly at each word. Cover it up and write it in the middle column. Use the techniques you have learned to try to remember the correct spelling of any words you spelt wrongly.
- Look quickly at each word. Cover it up and write the word again in the last column. Did you spell it correctly? If not, keep practising until you do.

acceptable		
accommodate		
calendar		
conscience		
conscious		
embarrass		
existence		
intelligence		
noticeable		
occurrence		
particularly		
receive		
separate		
unnecessary		
weird		

Extension Use the techniques you have learned to correct the spelling of five words you regularly misspell.

11 Secrets of the sea

In this unit, you will develop your vocabulary, practise using perfect and progressive tenses, compound and complex sentences, and persuasive language, make notes from research.

Adjectives of size

- Decide whether the adjectives of size below describe something very large or something particularly small.

colossal, diminutive, elephantine, enormous, gargantuan, giant, gigantic, huge, immense, infinitesimal, mammoth, massive, microscopic, miniature, miniscule, minute, mouse-like, tiny, titanic, vast

Large	Small

Perfect and progressive verb forms

The perfect and progressive verb forms are ways of expressing the state of something that is going on in the present or past tense. For example, in the past progressive sentence, 'The boys were playing football in the dark', 'were' is in the past tense but the action of 'playing' football is continued.

Similarly, a present perfect sentence maintains the idea that the action itself is over or not currently happening. For example, 'The boys had played football in the park that morning.'

It is also possible to combine these verb forms to create present perfect progressive and past perfect progressive sentences. For example, 'The boys had been playing football in the park that morning.'

- Write the verb phrases that make use of the perfect or progressive in the sentences below in the second column of the table. The sentences come from 'Monsters from the deep' on page 164 of your Student Book. State which tense they are.

The gigantic sea creature, at least 15 metres long, with razor-sharp hooks on the end of its tentacles, was feasting on a Patagonian toothfish when it was caught by New Zealand fishermen.	
They had been fishing with long lines for Patagonian toothfish when it was hauled from the deep.	

Extension Write your own examples of the present and past progressive, and the present and past perfect progressive.

Words starting with *man-*

The word 'manoeuvre' uses the Latin word *mani*.

- Find out the meaning of each of the following words that also use the Latin word *mani*. Write your definitions in the boxes below. What do you think the prefix *man-* means?
- See if you can find more words that start with *man-*. Example: 'manifestation'.

manacle	
manage	
manicure	
manifest	
manipulate	
manner	
manual	
manufacture	
manuscript	

Extension Find words starting with the prefixes *over-*, *mis-* and *inter-*. What meaning does each prefix add?

Vocabulary: sea creatures

- Match each type of sea creature with the correct definition.

butterfly fish	a shark with a rectangular, flattened head
coral	a flat fish with a whip-like tail
hammerhead	a small sea creature that swims upright
jellyfish	a variety of tropical fish with wing-like fins
moray eel	an Arctic whale with a long ivory tusk
narwhal	a big sea creature with a large brain
sea horse	a polyp that creates its own plant-like skeleton
sperm whale	an echinoderm with five arms
starfish	a long fish with teeth and no external fins
stingray	a marine invertebrate made of gelatinous material

Researching for an information comic strip

- Write the name of an ocean creature below and use the space to make notes for an information comic strip like the one on page 166 of your Student Book.

My chosen ocean creature:
What species are they?
Where do they live and what do they feed on?
Are there any environmental threats to their survival?
What interests you most about them?

Extension Draw a scale picture of your chosen ocean creature to include in your comic strip.

Result clauses

Result clauses are coordinate clauses that use the conjunction 'so' to explain the result of something stated in a related clause (usually a main clause).

- Match each main clause below with a result clause to construct four compound sentences that make sense.

Main clause
There had been a clean-up day to remove all the rubbish
It had rained all morning
The parking meter had run out of money
Some of the crowd had stayed behind at the end

Result clause
so I put more coins in it.
so that they could meet the players.
so the clothes on the line were soaking wet.
so that everyone could enjoy the park.

- Write four of your own 'so' clauses.

'Not only … but also' complex sentences

- Write three of your own sentences using the same construction as the example below.

Colossal squid are not only larger than giant squid but also meaner.

Sentences with 'since'

- Complete the sentences below using 'since' and your own ideas.

My cousin wasn't able to come on holiday with us since ______________________.

The family were forced to leave their home since ______________________.

Goldfish make good pets since ______________________.

I am able to go skiing this year since ______________________.

He has refused to pay the fine since ______________________.

Extension Write new sentences using 'since' and your own ideas.

Persuasive language

- Match each persuasive literary device to the correct example. Some examples use more than one technique.

repeated words
rule of three
alliterative words
emotional language
rhetorical questions
similes or metaphors
humour

Imagine the blissful excitement when you feel something big tug on the end of your hook.
What do you think about a fresh, flavoursome, fishy feast for dinner tonight?
Fish are easy to weigh because they have their own scales!
It's big, it's hooked and it's coming up!
It's a whale of a fish, as big as three fire engines all in a row.

- What literary device does each of these captions about food use?

Caption	Device
Grill and chill	
I'm soy into sushi.	
Good food, good company, good time	
This is a festival of flavours!	
Oh, did you say 'exercise'? I thought you said 'extra fries'.	

- Write your own persuasive paragraph to convince your reader that a fresh fish supper is the best meal ever.

Extension Write some persuasive sentences using 'not only ... but also' and 'since' forms. Example: '... not only is it the biggest but also the tastiest'.

12 Island living

In this unit, you will develop your vocabulary, revise using persuasive language and punctuation, and write an advert and a playscript.

Persuasive language in adverts

- Read the advert below describing an island holiday destination. Circle all the verbs and underline the adjectives.

Want to escape the humdrum of your busy life? Imagine sitting on warm, golden sand, sheltered by the cool shade of a palm tree, legs lazily outstretched, the soft, turquoise sea tickling the tip of your toes as you snooze in the sleepy sunshine. Sound appealing? Then Philamosa is the island retreat for you. Miles of unspoilt, sandy beaches, caressed by the tide of the blue sea like pristine pools of sapphires. This precious island is waiting for you.

- Match each of the verbs and adjectives with the correct definition.

precious	lightly touching to cause pleasure or mild discomfort
pristine	of great value
sheltered	in its original condition
snooze	protected from bad or extreme weather conditions
tickling	short light sleep
unspoilt	not changed or built upon recently

- Explain how the verb 'tickling' is used persuasively in the advert. Then explain how the rhetorical question 'Sound appealing?' is also used persuasively.

Extension Write a descriptive paragraph of your own and highlight the adjectives and verbs.

Using persuasive language

Writers use different techniques to persuade their readers.

- Match each persuasion technique with the correct example from the advert on page 77.

pun	for you
alliteration	blue sea like pristine pools of sapphires
simile	legs lazily … you snooze in the sleepy sunshine
personification	pristine pools of sapphires / This precious island
stimulating imagination	caressed by the tide
rhetorical questions	as you snooze in the sleepy sunshine
talking directly to reader	warm, golden sand, sheltered by the cool shade
repetition of an idea	Imagine sitting …
language appealing to different senses	Want to escape the humdrum of your busy city life?

- Write your own advert for an island holiday destination. Use your own words and some of the persuasion techniques above.

Extension Find a phrase in the advert on page 77 of this Workbook which uses both alliteration and personification at the same time.

Vocabulary

- Choose the correct words and phrases below to complete the sentences.

contaminated, poignant, profound, repressed, rite of passage, wary

There is a ____________________ moment in the film when Juan realizes the stranger is his father.
All the fish are dead because the river has been ____________________ by waste from the factory.
When he laughed at her, years of ____________________ anger suddenly boiled over inside her.
Learning to drive is a kind of ____________________ for young people in America.
Julia felt ____________________ of the stranger but didn't say anything to her friends.
Shakespeare made some very ____________________ observations about life in his plays that are still relevant today.

Words starting with *out-*

- Match each word starting with *out-* with the correct definition.

outcry	a person who has committed a crime but not been caught yet
outdated	letting opinions be known even if those opinions are quite shocking
outdoors	defeat or get the better of someone by being clever
outlaw	in the open air; outside a building or shelter
outsmart	a strong expression of public disapproval or anger
outspoken	old-fashioned, no longer relevant

- Write a sentence using each of the words below.

outcry	
outdated	
outdoors	
outlaw	
outsmart	
outspoken	

Punctuation

- This is a book review of *Treasure Island*. Fill the gaps with the correct punctuation.

To immerse yourself in pure swashbuckling adventure ___ look no further ___ *Treasure Island* ___ Robert Louis Stevenson, 1883 ___ is the perfect pirate story. The list of main characters includes ___ the young Jim Hawkins who holds the treasure map ___ the sinister blind Pew who first encountered Jim ___ Ben Gunn, a reformed pirate, known as 'The man of the island', who was marooned on the island three years before the story takes place ___ and the other main protagonist of the book ___ the legendary Long John Silver ___ a villainous rogue who sets the tone of this tale of treachery ___ greed and courage. From his first encounter with pirates ___ right through to the climactic battle for treasure on Treasure Island ___ the narrative paints colourful scenes and grotesque characters that have fired the imaginations of generations of readers ___ it is the story of good triumphing over evil ___

Identifying features of a prose text

- Read the extract below from *Treasure Island*. Highlight any description of characters or action and underline any dialogue.

He was plainly blind, for he tapped before him with a stick, and wore a great, green shade over his eyes and nose; and he was hunched, as if with age or weakness, and wore a huge old, tattered sea-cloak with a hood. I never saw in my life a more dreadful-looking figure. He stopped a little way from me, and, raising his voice in an odd sing-song, addressed the air in front of him: – "Will any kind friend inform a poor blind man, who has lost the precious sight of his eyes in the gracious defence of his native country, – where or in what part of this country he may now be?" "You are at Black Hill Cove, my good man," said I. "I hear a voice," said he – "a young voice. Will you give me your hand, my kind young friend, and lead me in?" I held out my hand, and the horrible, soft-spoken creature gripped it in a moment like a vice. I was so much startled that I struggled to withdraw; but the blind man pulled me close up to him with a single action of his arm. "Now, boy," he said, "take me in to the captain." "Sir," said I, "upon my word I dare not." "Oh," he sneered, "Take me straight to him, or I'll break your arm." And he gave it, as he spoke, a wrench that made me cry out. "Come, now, march," and I never heard a voice so cruel, and cold, and ugly as that blind man's.

Writing a playscript

- Rewrite the narrative on the previous page into playscript form. Remember to add stage directions as well as the characters' dialogue.

(A blind, hunched old man walks towards the boy tapping a stick before him. He is wearing ...

Extension Write your own paragraph. Include at least one of each of the following: a dash, brackets, a colon, a semi-colon and an exclamation mark.

Cross-curricular words to help you at school

Here are all the cross-curricular words you are learning this year. Highlight any words you don't know and read the definitions. Use this list for reference as you complete the activities on the following pages.

advantage *noun* something useful or helpful
'In this game, being tall is an advantage'.

alternative *noun* one of two or more things that you can choose between
'I looked for a vegetarian alternative on the menu.'
adjective available instead of something else
'The road was flooded so we had to return by an alternative route.'

anecdote *noun* a short, amusing or interesting story about a real person or thing
'The teacher started the lesson by sharing an amusing anecdote.'

benefit *noun* an advantage that something brings
'His height was a great benefit for playing basketball.'
verb to give an advantage to someone or something
'The newly built park will benefit children living in the community'.

characterize *verb* to be a characteristic of someone or something
'Bright colours characterize his paintings.'

contemplate *verb* to consider or think about doing something
'Did you ever contemplate living in another country?'

contradict *verb* to say that something said is not true or that someone is wrong; to say the opposite of
'The two newspaper reports totally contradict each other.'

contrast *noun* a difference clearly seen when things are compared
'I like the contrast of the yellow curtains with the blue bed cover.'
verb to compare two things in order to show that they are clearly different
'It's interesting to contrast the styles of these two writers.'

defy *verb* to resist something openly; to refuse to obey something
'If we defy the ban on single-use plastics, the environment will suffer.'

delicate *adjective* 1. of fine quality or craftsmanship
'Her wedding dress was made from very delicate lace.'
2. fragile and easily damaged
'Peaches have delicate skins.'

display *verb* 1. to show or arrange something so that it can be seen
'The exhibition gives local artists the opportunity to display their work.'
2. to show a particular quality or emotion
'They displayed great courage during the wildfire.'

domestic *adjective* to do with your house, home or family
'Everyone has domestic chores they need to do from time to time.'

empathy *noun* being able to understand and share in the feelings of another person
'I felt real empathy towards the people who had lost their homes.'

exemplify *verb* to be an example of something
'This painting perfectly exemplifies the impressionist style.'

exhibit *noun* an object or work of art on display in a gallery or museum
'The museum's exhibits range from Iron Age pottery to Inuit clothing.'

verb to show or display something in public
'The artist exhibits his paintings in several galleries.'

extravagant *adjective* spending too much money or using too many resources
'We are going on a less extravagant holiday this year.'

focus *noun* something that is a centre of interest or attention
'He could be successful, but he lacks focus.'

verb to concentrate on something
'If you focus in class, you will pass your exams.'

freedom *noun* the fact of being free; independence
'Freedom is the main theme in this novel.'

honour *noun* great respect or reputation
'You must show honour to your family.'

hostility *noun* unfriendly and aggressive behaviour or actions
'There was an edge of hostility in his voice.'

independence *noun* the freedom to live your life without being dependent on someone else
'The country gained its independence ten years ago.'

indicate *verb* to point something out or make it known
'Please indicate clearly which colour you require.'

interpretation *noun* explaining what something means
'I didn't understand his interpretation of the poem.'

perspective *noun* 1. a person's particular opinion or point of view about something
'I have changed my perspective on the importance of regular exercise.'

2. a good understanding of how important different things are
'It is important to put these difficulties into perspective.'

reject *verb* to refuse to accept a person or thing
'I was afraid that my teacher would reject my excuse for being late.'

relationship *noun* the way in which people or things are connected or related to one another
'I have quite a good relationship with my parents.'

responsible *adjective* legally or morally obliged to take care of something or to carry out a duty, and having to take the blame if something goes wrong
'Pilots are responsible for their passengers' safety.'

significant *adjective* 1. having a meaning; full of meaning
'My first trip overseas was a very significant moment in my life.'

2. important, substantial
'I made a significant saving on the train fare.'

source *noun* the person, place or thing from which something comes
'The fire was the only source of light in the room.'

specific *adjective* definite or precise; to do with a particular thing
'Please be more specific about your holiday plans.'

speculation *noun* forming opinions without having any definite evidence
'There was much speculation about the cause of the fire.'

synonym *noun* a word that means the same or almost the same as another word
'The teacher told us to use synonyms in our writing.'

testimony *noun* evidence; what someone testifies
'According to his testimony, he was nowhere near the scene of the crime.'

Practice

1 Match the underlined words in each sentence to the word with a similar meaning.

When I leave home, I will be able have a lot more <u>freedom</u>.	reject
Thank you for making such a <u>great</u> contribution to our fundraising efforts.	independence
There has been a lot of <u>talk</u> about which famous actor will play the character in the film.	advantage
My opponent was injured during the match, giving me an <u>aid</u> in my attempt to win.	speculation
Although his offer is very generous, I am going to <u>refuse</u> it.	significant

2 Fill in the missing words in each sentence with one of the words below.
defy, perspective, relationship, anecdote, display, hostility

a I have a good ________________ with all my colleagues, which makes the job really enjoyable.
b She is getting too upset over a small matter and needs to put things into ________________.
c I am going to choose my three favourite pictures and ________________ them on the wall.
d My aunt travels a lot and she told me a fascinating ________________ about her latest trip.
e Her attitude towards me swings between friendship and ________________.
f I would never dare to ________________ my teachers.

3 Write sentences of your own using each of the words below.
contemplate, alternative, responsible, honour, indicate, interpretation

a ____
b ____
c ____
d ____
e ____
f ____

4 Find synonyms (words with the same meaning) and antonyms (words with the opposite meaning) of the words in the grid and add them to the appropriate column. Try to think of as many of each as you can.

	Synonym	**Antonym**
exemplify	illustrate	cover, conceal
focus		
freedom		
benefit		
delicate		
testimony		

5 How many new words can you make from these words? You can add or remove letters, find words within words, and add prefixes or suffixes. Then write sentences using the new words.

extravagant	
specific	
domestic	
source	
contrast	
synonym	

6 Fill in the speech bubbles using one of the words from the box in each bubble. You can change the form of the word to make it fit, for example, "Let's decide who is going to play the main character." You can make the speech bubbles as funny or unusual as you like. Work with a partner and use your imagination. Use a dictionary or the internet to help with spelling.

characterize **contradict** **empathy**

7 Now it's time to get really creative!

If you are working with a partner:

- Choose **six** words from the list on pages 82–84 that you think are the most useful.
- Take turns to explain a word to your partner, describing it, but WITHOUT SAYING THE WORD.

If you are working alone:

- Choose **six** words from the list on pages 82–84 that you think are the most useful.
- Write a story of your choice using the six words. You can add prefixes and suffixes to the words as well.
- The images below are to help give you ideas for your story.

8 You are going to write a news report on a subject of your choice. In the report, you must include at least **six** cross-curricular words. You can either write them in the box below before you begin, or decide on the words as you write and then add them to the box.

-
-
-
-
-
-

Grammar and language terms

abstract noun an abstract noun identifies things which cannot be physically touched or seen, such as a state, idea, process or feeling
'My dream is to make progress.'

active voice a set of verb forms in which the subject of a verb performs the action
'The dog is chasing the cat.'

adjectival phrase a group of words containing an adjective that describes a noun or a pronoun
'The cat had vivid green eyes.'

adverbial a word or phrase which gives more information about a verb or a clause. An adverbial can be an adverb, a phrase or a subordinate clause.
Adverbials tell you where, when, why, how or how often something was done.
'The dog slept under the table.'
'I usually do my homework before I watch TV.'
'Jack worked very hard.'
'The cat sleeps all day.'
Adverbials sometimes appear at the beginning of a sentence. These are called 'fronted adverbials'. There is usually a comma after a fronted adverbial.
'First thing in the morning, I walk the dog.'
'Next, I have my breakfast.'
Some adverbials link ideas across paragraphs or within paragraphs. These adverbials are often fronted and are usually followed by a comma.
'on the other hand'; 'in contrast'; 'as a result'; 'secondly'

alliteration occurs when two or more nearby words start with the same sound
'A slow, sad, sorrowful song.'

anthropomorphism giving human characteristics, emotions or behaviours to animals, things and gods. Characters like Simba and the other talking lions from *The Lion King*, the Cheshire Cat, the Caterpillar and the White Rabbit from *Alice in Wonderland*, and the gods from Greek mythology are examples of anthropomorphism.

auxiliary verbs these are used with main verbs to indicate continuous actions or to form different tenses. 'Be' and 'have' are auxiliary verbs.
'I am eating.'
'It has rained all night.'
The auxiliary verb 'do' is used in negative statements, questions and commands.
'I do not want any more chocolate.'
'Do you want some?'
'Do sit still!'

clause a group of words that contains a subject and a verb. Every full sentence contains at least one main clause.
'I ran.' (In this clause, 'I' is the subject and 'ran' is the verb.)

Multi-clause sentences contain one or more subordinate clauses. A subordinate clause does not make sense on its own and relies on the main clause.
'When I had finished reading it, I returned the book to the library.'
(In this sentence, the clause 'When I had finished reading it' is a subordinate clause, which depends on the main clause, 'I returned the book to the library', to make sense.)

comparative comparative adjectives are used when two things are being compared
'Morning break is only fifteen minutes, but the lunch break is longer.'
'My brother finds maths more difficult than English.'

concrete noun a concrete noun identifies things which can be physically seen or touched
'Lizzie ate her toast in the kitchen.'

conditional (relating to) a sentence in which one part expresses something which depends on the other part. Conditional sentences often begin 'if' or 'unless'.
'If I win this race, I will get a prize.'

conjugation the way a verb conjugates. To conjugate a verb means to give all the different forms of a verb according to tense and person.

conjunction a word used to link words or clauses within a sentence
'and'; 'but'; 'so'; 'until'; 'when'; 'as'
'He was running when he went to the shops.'

conjunctive adverb a type of adverb that joins two clauses in a sentence, creating a link between them. Conjunctive adverbs can also show the cause and effect of an action.
'accordingly'; 'also'; 'besides'; 'consequently'; 'finally'; 'however'; 'indeed'; 'instead'

contraction when an apostrophe is used to show that letters have been removed from a word
'didn't' (for 'did not'); 'it's' (for 'it is')

coordinate clause a coordinate clause is made when you connect two short clauses that are of equal importance. These clauses are connected by coordinating conjunctions such as 'for', 'and', 'nor', 'but', 'or', 'yet', and 'so'.
'Rajiv went into town and bought a new football.'

determiner a word like 'a', 'the', 'some', 'any', 'my', 'each', 'every', 'either' and 'no' which is used before a noun, or at the start of a noun phrase. Determiners tell you which one, how many or how much.
'The girls enjoyed the music.'
'There is a bird on the branch.'
'Each box contained 20 books.'

dialogue an oral or written conversation

direct speech when speech marks are used to show that someone is speaking
"Can I talk to you please?" asked Sam.

dynamic verb a verb used primarily to indicate an action, process or sensation as opposed to a state
'The dog jumped over the wall.'

exclamation a type of sentence indicating strong feelings and emotions

exclamation mark an exclamation mark (!) is used to indicate shouting, surprise or excitement in direct speech. It can also be used after an order or instruction, or to express surprise, alarm or excitement in a narrative.
"Wow!" exclaimed Maria. "That's a real mammoth's tooth!"
'Get down from that table this instant!'
'Someone was coming. She must hurry!'

expanded noun phrase a noun phrase that has a noun as its head, or key word: 'ball' (noun); 'the ball' (noun phrase). Expanded noun phrases add more detail to the noun by adding one or more adjectives or by saying where the noun is.
'the red pencil on the floor by the desk'

figurative language figurative language uses words for the effects they create, rather than their literal meanings. It often produces vivid images and sounds in the mind of the reader or listener. The most common types of figurative language are: simile, metaphor, personification, hyperbole and onomatopoeia.
'This homework will take forever!' (hyperbole)
'My hands are as cold as ice.' (simile)
'Her eyes blazed with anger.' (metaphor)

fronted if a word or phrase is fronted, it has been moved to the front of a clause. For example, in the sentence 'Later that day, I saw him again', 'later that day' is a fronted phrase or a fronted adverbial.

fronted adverbial sometimes adverbials appear at the beginning of a sentence. These are called 'fronted adverbials'. There is usually a comma after a fronted adverbial.
'First thing in the morning, I walk the dog.'
'Next, I have my breakfast.'

fronted conditional clause a conditional clause, usually beginning with 'if' or 'unless', which comes before the main clause
'Unless you have your passport with you, you will not be permitted to fly.'

genre a type of writing. Poetry, fantasy and non-fiction are examples of different genres.

homograph homographs are words that are spelled the same way but not necessarily pronounced the same way and have different meanings and origins
Spelled the same way but pronounced differently:
'A tear rolled down Sasha's cheek.'
'Tear the form off and send it to the address below.'
Spelled and pronounced the same:
'The head teacher rose from her seat.'
'The ball landed in the rose bushes.'

homophone one of two or more words that sound the same but have different meanings. They may have the same or different spellings.
'right' and 'write'; 'meat' and 'meet'

idiom a colourful expression that cannot be understood from the meaning of its separate words
'It's raining cats and dogs.' (This means that it is raining very hard.)

imperative the form of the verb used to make commands
'Go away!'

indirect speech speech that has been reported but not in the exact words or in quotation marks; also called reported speech

infinitive the form of a verb that does not change to indicate a particular tense or number or person. In English, it is used with or without 'to' (the verb form without the 'to' is often called the **root form**). For example, 'sing' in 'I want to sing' and 'go' in 'Let me go'.

intransitive verb a verb that does not have a direct object after it
'see' in 'we can see' (but not in 'we can see you', which has an object ('you') and is **transitive**)

irregular verb any verb that does not follow the expected pattern of conjugation in some way. In English, this is usually by not adding *-ed* or *-d* to its past tense form.
'go' (went); 'is' (was); 'do' (did); 'eat' (ate); 'get' (got); 'have' (had); 'make' (made)

main verb the most important verb in the sentence. It describes the action or state of the subject of the sentence.
'The children climbed the tree.'
'We ate a large bar of chocolate during the film.'

metaphor a way of speaking or writing in which one thing is said to be something else. This way of speaking or writing is called a figure of speech.
'Thanks for your help. You are a star!'

metaphorical language any form of language that makes use of metaphor

modal verb modal verbs are used with a verb to show what is possible, or necessary, or what is going to happen (including 'could', 'should', must', 'shall', 'may', 'might', 'will' and 'would')
'I should go for a walk.'
'I can lend you my textbook if you need it.'

multi-clause sentence a sentence that consists of more than one clause
'The girl ran to her mother because she was afraid of the dog.'

negation a statement that cancels out or denies another statement or action
'I don't know where the treasure is.'

noun phrase a small group of words containing a noun or pronoun and one or more modifiers
'the little boy', 'my green sports bag'

passive voice verb forms in which the subject of the sentence is the person or thing affected by the verb. It is formed using the **auxiliary verb** 'be' and the **past participle**.
'A window was broken.'

participle a word formed from a verb (e.g. 'gone' and 'going' from the verb 'to go'; 'guided' and 'guiding' from the verb 'to guide') and used with an auxiliary verb to form certain tenses. See **past participle** and **present participle**.

past participle the past participle (e.g. 'gone', 'guided') describes a completed action or past condition. See also **participle**. Past participles can be used as adjectives, for example 'the burnt toast', or 'the broken pencil'.

perfect verb forms these express a completed action or state. They are the opposite of progressive verb forms (which tell us something is or was continuing at the time). We use the perfect tenses to show that the action has finished and is no longer continuing.
'We have already eaten.'
'He had painted the front door.'

personification the technique of giving human qualities to things that are not human, such as an animal, concept or inanimate object
'The sun beamed happily while the kittens played hide-and-seek, and life danced by.'

phrasal verb an expression using a verb combined with a preposition and/or an adverb. In a phrasal verb, the individual words often do not have their usual meaning.
'Please look after your little brother.'
'He went off down the road.'

possessive determiners are used with a noun, to show who or what it belongs to or is related to, for example: 'my', 'your', 'his', 'her', 'its', 'our' and 'their'
'Is it okay to wear my trainers?'

possessive pronouns these tell you who owns the thing you are talking about or who is involved in the process or action. Possessive pronouns are used instead of the noun, for example: 'mine', 'yours', 'his', 'hers', 'ours' and 'theirs'.
'Is that school jumper mine or yours?'

prefix a word or syllable placed at the beginning of a word to modify its meaning. For example, In the word 'misunderstand', the prefix *mis-* makes the word 'understand' mean 'not understand correctly'. In the word 'unhappy', the prefix *un-* makes the word 'happy' mean 'not happy'.

preposition a word that indicates place ('on', 'in'), direction ('over', 'beyond') or time ('during', 'on') among others
'I read my book during lunch. I put the book in the drawer.'

present participle this is usually formed by adding *-ing* to the infinitive of the verb. See also **participle**.
Present participles are sometimes used as adjectives.
'It has been an exciting day.'
Present participles are sometimes used as nouns.
'Swimming is a popular sport.'

progressive verb forms these express an action or state of being that is ongoing and not yet completed. The **present participle** is used to indicate this with the **auxiliary verb** 'be'.
'They are still eating.'
'He was painting the front door.'

pronoun a word that can replace a noun
'I'; 'me'; 'mine'; 'myself'

relative clause a type of subordinate clause introduced using the relative pronouns 'that', 'which', 'who', 'whom', and 'whose'
'The film that we watched yesterday was very exciting.'

result clause a type of subordinate clause that shows the result of an action or situation. Result clauses help answer the question of why something happened. They are introduced by conjunctions such as 'so', 'so … that', and 'such … that'.

root form of a verb this is the same as the infinitive, but without 'to'. For example, in the verb 'to eat', 'eat' is the root form (also called the base form).

sentence functions when we describe a sentence based on its function, we are talking about its purpose. There are four types of function: statement, question, command and exclamation.

simile a figure of speech in which two things are compared using the linking words 'like' or 'as'
'In battle, he was <u>as brave as a lion</u>.'
'He behaves <u>like a brave lion</u>.'

simple present tense used when an action is happening at the present moment, or when it happens regularly. Depending on the person, the simple present tense is formed by using the **root form of the verb** or by adding *-s* or *-es* to the end.
'He <u>gets</u> up very early every morning.'

statement spoken or written words that give facts or express an opinion

stative verb stative verbs describe a state rather than an action. Common examples include 'be', 'have', 'like', 'seem', 'prefer', 'understand', 'belong', 'doubt', 'hate' and 'know'.

subordinate clause a clause which adds details to the main clause of the sentence but cannot be used as a sentence by itself
'<u>When I finish my homework</u>, I will go and meet my friends.'

suffix a word or syllable placed at the end of a word to modify its meaning. For example, in the word 'tasteless', the suffix *-less* makes the word 'tasteless' mean 'with no taste'.

superlative superlative adjectives and adverbs are used to compare and contrast three or more people, things or actions. The superlative shows which is greatest or most, and is generally formed by adding *-est* or *-st*.
'Cheetahs are <u>the fastest</u> land animals.'

syllable a unit of pronunciation that forms part of or the whole of a word. English words consist of one or more syllables. Each syllable always contains one speech vowel. This may have one or more speech consonants before and/or after it.
1 syllable – 'house', 2 syllables – 'kettle', 3 syllables – 'butterfly'

synonym a word or phrase that means exactly or nearly the same as another word or phrase in the same language. For example, the verb 'shut' is a synonym of the verb 'close'.

transitive verb a transitive verb is used with a direct object after it
'I must change my shoes.' ('shoes' are the object of the verb 'changes')

verb phrase a group of words, including the main verb and any other linking verbs or modifiers, that act as a sentence's verb
'My brother <u>is studying</u> in his room.'